When You Work For a Jerk

Techniques to Survive an Evil Boss and
Work Your Way to the Top

By K.C. Smith

Copyright 2017 by K.C. Smith

Published by Make Profits Easy LLC

Profitsdaily123@aol.com

facebook.com/MakeProfitsEasy

Table of Contents

Introduction 5

Chapter 1: Five Types of Bad Bosses 9

Chapter 2: Emotional Intelligence 16

Chapter 3: Less is More 27

Chapter 4: Reputation 33

Chapter 5: Remain Positive 37

Chapter 6: Stress Relieving Methods 45

Chapter 7: Stay One Step Ahead of The Game .. 52

Chapter 8: See the Bigger Picture 57

Chapter 9: Remain Immune To Your Bosses Behavior 61

Chapter 10: Improve Your Communication Skills 67

Chapter 11: Improve Your Conflict Resolution Skills 72

Chapter 12: How to cope when your boss is a bully 88

Chapter 13: How to motivate yourself in the workplace 93

Chapter 14: Don't Outshine Your Boss 99

Chapter 15: If All Else Fails, Kill Them With Kindness 109

Conclusion.. 115

Introduction

Whether you work on Wall Street or in McDonalds, no employee wants to have to deal with a bad boss. Cantankerous managers contaminate the workplace; they are the reason why you hate Monday's and love Fridays. Some bosses are blatant about their quest for power and they wear the "jerk" label with zero shame. Where as other managers are a bit more manipulative about it and covertly use their employees to get what they want. Regardless of how they choose to spill their venom, a bad boss can cause irreversible damage to a company and its employees by stagnating performance and creating undue stress.

A boss who antagonizes their employees is bad for the health. There have been several studies which have discovered that working under bad management can increase your chances of heart failure by up to 50 percent.

Even more disturbing is the number of tyrant bosses out there. A Gallup poll discovered that 60 percent of government workers were down in the dumps because of bad management. Another study found that 69 percent of workers in the United States compared managers with too much power to toddlers given the permission to do what they want! Now we all know what happens when you let a toddler do what they want, they destroy the place....... Not good!

The comparisons don't end there. A large number of employees in America describe their bosses in the following terms:

- Self absorbed – 60 percent
- Stuck in their ways 49 percent
- Too demanding - 43 percent
- Impulsive – 41 percent
- Disruptive - 39 percent

When a group of managers were showed these statistics they were surprised and concerned at the same time that employees had such a negative view of management. A DDI study discovered that 64 percent of managers are aware that they need to make improvements on their management ability. When asked what areas they think need the most improvement, the majority of them responded with, "making the numbers." However, an overwhelming number of managers lose their jobs because of poor people skills.

TalentSmart has spent years conducting research on more than 1 million people, and found that 90% of high achievers are skilled at keeping their emotions under control during stressful situations. One of their best assets is their ability to countervail toxic people – even those who are in positions of authority over them. This is not an easy task and it requires a high level of emotional intelligence, which is a skill that high achievers rely on.

Instead of dealing with a toxic boss, the majority of employees leave and seek employment elsewhere. However, with the current economic climate it isn't always that easy. Also it does not look good on your resume when you have had too many jobs. Successful people know how turn a negative situation into a positive one, a bad manager has no effect on them because they have the understanding that success manifests as a result of how skilfully you can play the hand that you have been dealt. When that hand is a toxic boss, a high achiever will identify the type of boss they are working with and then use the information that they gather to neutralize their behavior.

This book will provide you with proven techniques on how to survive an evil boss.

Chapter 1: Five Types of Bad Bosses

The first step in surviving an evil boss is to identify who they are and according to research there are five types:

1. **The Divider**

    The divisive boss has favorites, but what the favorites fail to realize is that they are not on the boss's side because they are genuinely liked. A favorite is often weak and easy to manipulate, the boss will use them to gather information about what is taking place in the workplace. Which employees are cutting corners, who is talking about them etc. The bad thing about this type of divisive boss is that all the other employees are aware that they have a favorite and it can cause friction in the workplace which inevitably has a negative effect on productivity.

Another type of divisive manager is the one who was promoted from within a certain team. He or she still takes lunch breaks with their friends on the team which excludes the other workers.

Several surveys have reported that playing favorites is the number one complaint against management.

Experts claim that this style of management is a personality issue. Managers of this nature usually wanted to be a part of the in-crowd when they were in high school and have carried that behavior into the workplace.

2. The micromanager

Possibly the worst type of manager you could get! Someone who sits looking over your shoulder and has to check every two words that you write. When you are confident in your abilities, this type of manager can be really off putting. You can have the most talented team in the world, but the micromanager is constantly hovering over them like a bad smell making sure the work is done the way they would do it. It's this type of boss that makes you want to throw in the towel and just say "do it yourself then!"

A micromanager can make you feel as if you can't be trusted and are constantly telling you what to do and when to do it. You are made to feel as if you are back in college and have just started your first job.

3. By the numbers

The opposite of a micromanager is the boss who is so focused on reports and analytics that the staff are not given the direction that they need. This type of manager is detached from the people they are managing. They may be good in every other area but they lack people skills.

While this type of management style might work for top performers who don't need much guidance, it doesn't work for employees who need more support. Often a boss of this nature unwittingly gives their power to an employee who then takes on an informal leadership role which leads to resentment within the team.

Managers of this nature are often insecure in their roll as a leader and so put all their energy into numbers because that is what they are comfortable with. This type of leadership often results in a high turnover which can put a strain on the financial resources of an organization. Employees will leave not necessarily because the manager is bad but because they need direction. The majority of employees are not entrepreneurs and require instruction to function effectively.

4. The Workaholic

A workaholic boss is the type who stays up all night to get the work done and expects everyone else to be the same. They will email their employees at 2am expecting a response and get angry when they don't get one immediately. They are renowned for dishing out last minute assignments and expecting their employees to drop what they are doing to get it done or to stay in the office after hours to complete the project.

It is highly inappropriate for a manager to expect their staff to work around the clock. What they will find is that this type of management style is ineffective in the long run because it leads to burn out and causes employees to become disengaged.

A boss like this is often forward thinking, they have already exceeded targets for the quarter that they are in and they are already trying to meet targets for the next quarter!

5. **The bully**

A bully boss uses public humiliation and intimidation to make sure that their employees don't step out of line not realizing that their behavior typically has the opposite effect. This type of manager abuses the power and authority they have been given over their employees. They will often use bad language and shout at their employees in public.

If you are working in an environment where you have to deal with a manager that fits any of the above categories, first I would like to express my condolences! However, before you decide to hand in your resignation the truth of the matter is that a good manager is hard to find, so it is more than likely that you will run into the same if not worse at your next job! Therefore, the best way to deal with this is to learn how to neutralize such character traits and use them to your advantage.

Chapter 2: Emotional Intelligence

Shout, scream, pound your fists against the wall, have endless conversations about how to assassinate your boss although you know you don't have the guts to do so! All of this is a complete waste of energy so why not try something else.

One things for certain and two things for sure you can't change people, but you can change yourself. One of the most effective methods of handling negative situations in general is to have a high level of emotional intelligence. (EI)

It is more than likely that you know someone either in your personal life or at work who is a great listener. Regardless of what is happening in their life, they always say the right thing at the right time; they say the right things in the right way so that we don't get upset or offended. They are considerate and caring, and even if we leave without a solution to the problem, we feel more optimistic and hopeful that we will find one.

You may know someone who is an expert at controlling their emotions. They don't react the way everyone else does when they are in negative situations. Instead, they take a step back, analyze the problem and then calmly work towards finding a solution. They have got excellent decision making skills and know when to put their trust in their intuition and when not to. They are always willing to honestly evaluate themselves and they use criticism as a stepping stone to self improvement instead of getting offended by it.

People of this nature have a high level of emotional intelligence. They know exactly who they are and they are also in tune with the needs and emotions of those around them. Wouldn't you want to be more like this?

As more organizations are starting to accept that EI goes hand in hand with professional success and that it is equally as important as technical ability, companies are now starting to measure the EI of the people they promote or hire.

For example, a large cosmetics company changed their hiring process by basing it on selecting candidates with a high level of EI. They found that the new salespeople hired using this method sold on average $91,000 more than those who were recruited under the old system. They also found that the new group of salespeople had a significantly lower staff turnover then other salespeople within the company.

So what exactly is emotional intelligence, and what steps can you take to improve yours?

Emotional Intelligence

Every one of us is unique, our personalities are different, our needs, wants and desires are different, and the way we show our emotions are different. If you want to succeed in life, manoeuvring through this takes cleverness and tact, this is where EI becomes effective.

In short, emotional intelligence is the ability to handle your emotions. You are capable of understanding what they are telling you at any given moment and you are aware of how they affect others around you. It also involves how you perceive others, when you are capable of understanding how others feel without them having to tell you it causes them to be more receptive towards you which in turn helps you to manage your relationships better.

People with high levels of EI are typically successful in every area of their life. Why? Because they are the type of people who everyone wants on their team. When people with a high EI need something done, it gets done, when they send emails, people answer. Not because they have special powers that no one else has but because they make people feel good. Life is much easier for them because they don't go through life getting angry over the smallest mishap.

Emotional Intelligence Characteristics

In 1995, American psychologist Daniel Goleman wrote a book entitled "Emotional Intelligence – Why it can matter more than IQ." In his book, he defined the five elements of emotional intelligence.

1. **Self Aware:** People with a high level of EI have an in-depth understanding of who they are. They are in control of their emotions and don't allow their feelings to affect their behavior.

   They are capable of critically evaluating themselves; they don't need someone else to do it for them. They are confident in their strengths, but also understand their weaknesses and they find ways to improve in these areas. Self awareness is said to be the most important aspect of EI.

2. **Self Regulation:** This is centered around a person's ability to control impulses and emotions. People who regulate themselves, don't allow emotions such as jealousy or anger to overtake them, neither do they make careless and impulsive decisions. Everything they do is

thought about carefully before they act. The characteristics of self regulation are integrity, thoughtfulness, having the ability to say no and being comfortable with change.

3. **Motivation:** They are highly productive and forward thinking. Immediate gratification is not something they indulge in because they are willing to put off short term satisfaction for long term success. Their motivation levels are high, they enjoy a challenge and they are successful in everything that they do.

4. **Social Skills:** People with good social skills are usually team players. Such people are likeable characters and they are easy to talk to. They would rather help someone else to develop and grow then focus on their own success. They have superior communication skills and they are excellent at conflict resolution. They

have mastered the art of maintaining and building relationships.

5. **Empathy:** This is another very important element of EI. The ability to understand and identify the needs, wants and viewpoints of those around you. They are good at recognizing people's feelings although they may not be obvious to everyone else. Empathetic people are typically good at managing relationships, they listen well and relate well with others. They don't stereotype or judge people without getting to know them first. They live very open and honest lives.

As I am sure you have realized from this information, EI is one of several keys to success in life and especially in your career. The ability to manage relationships and people is a very important characteristic in leaders. If you want to get ahead in your company even with a tyrant of a boss start improving your emotional intelligence.

Developing Your Emotional Intelligence

The good news is that if you were not born with a high EI you can develop one. Everybody has emotions, but it is what we do with them that will differentiate you from others. As well as developing your skills in the five above areas, you should also implement the following strategies.

- Observe your reactions towards others. Do you make quick judgments before you have been given all the facts? Do you make judgments based on stereotypes? Take a good honest look at how you interact with people, trade places with them and ask yourself if you would like you if you were them?
- Are you an attention seeker? Are you the type of person who has to get a pat on the back for everything that they do? Humility

is one of the best qualities that you can develop. I find this to be an interesting dichotomy, no one likes people who are constantly showing off and who always need attention. But on the other hand we are obsessed with celebrity lifestyles, we spend hours watching reality TV or flicking through magazines to get a glimpse of the lives of the rich and famous when all they are doing is flaunting their wealth to get attention. But when people you know actually act like that, it's annoying. Sounds like an alter ego to me! Humble people don't need to flaunt their accomplishments, they know who they are, they are confident in their abilities and don't need people telling them how great they are every five minutes.

- Evaluate yourself and make a note of your strengths and weakness. Can you come to terms with the fact that you are not perfect and that there are aspects of your character that you can improve upon? If you want to become a better person, self evaluation is something that you are going to have to do.

- How do you react when you are in a stressful situation? Do you get upset and angry immediately? How do you react when you don't get what you want, when you have to wait, or someone doesn't agree with your way of doing things? Do you play the blame game even if it isn't the other persons fault to make yourself feel better? The ability to stay calm in stressful situations is a quality that is valued in and outside of the business world. Learn how to control your emotions when things don't happen the way you expected them to.

- Learn how to take responsibility for what you do. If you offend someone, apologize to them. Don't trivialize what you have done and ignore the person you have upset. People are generally more forthcoming in accepting an apology when an honest attempt is made to resolve the issue.

- Before you do anything, evaluate how your choices will affect those around you. Put yourself in place of the people who you are likely to affect, how would you feel if this was done to you? If after carefully thinking about your decision, you have no choice but to move to implementation phase start working on how you can help others to handle the effects.

Once you have mastered the principles of EI, everything else will fall into place. Let's continue to look at ways that you can survive in the workplace when you have an evil boss.

Chapter 3: Less is More

No matter which type of boss you have they have observed your character. They may not have the best people skills but be very certain; they are very familiar with their employees. If you have the bully boss, have you not noticed that there is a certain type of person they victimize? The one who they know is not going to defend themselves, they wear their feelings on their forehead, everyone knows to tread carefully around Alley because if you say the wrong thing she might burst into tears!

Your goal is to be inconspicuous and you can achieve this by speaking less. Let's find out why this is such a good tactic to run rings around your evil boss.

In many ways power is a game of appearances and when you say less than you need to, you appear more powerful then you actually are. Have you ever been in a meeting and there are those few employees who don't know when to shut up?! They are so hell bent on proving they that they understand the inner workings of the organization that they monopolize the entire meeting. Please refrain from being that person, or if you are that person stop it now!

In general people don't like silence, when there is a group of people in the room, someone always has to say something to break the silence even if it's something completely ridiculous and the person just embarrasses themselves. This is because silence makes people uncomfortable, why is a book in itself so we won't go there. However, humans are machines of explanation and interpretation and they always want to know what you are thinking or how you are feeling. When you have control over what you reveal, people are unable to have access to your meaning and interpretation of any given situation.

Your silence and short answers will put them on the defensive and they will nervously jump in making comments and small talk that will reveal their weaknesses and valuable information about them. This tactic works well during an employee evaluation with guess who? Your evil boss! There are questions that you are going to have to answer, but be as vague as possible, and don't give away too much information. They will leave the meeting with you feeling as if you robbed them of something and will go home thinking about every word that you gave them the privilege of hearing. This extra attention they give to your comments will only enhance your power.

Saying less than is necessary is not only for statesmen and kings. It is a general rule in all areas of life, the less you say, the more mysterious and profound you appear. As a young artist, Andy Warhol became frustrated with his position and came to the conclusion that it was not possible to get people to do what you want by telling them what to do. He found that most of the time they resented being given instruction and would often turn against him. Warhol later told a friend that he has learnt that there is more power in silence then in speech. Later on in his life he used this same strategy and became very successful because of it. During his interviews he would say something ambiguous and vague and the interviewer would go around the world and back attempting to work out the profound meaning behind his often empty statements. Warhol spent little time talking about his work, he allowed other people to form their own opinions and interpret it themselves. He came to the conclusion that the less he spoke about his work, the more people became intrigued about it meaning that he didn't need to talk about it because other people were.

The more you speak, the more you risk saying something that could potentially harm you. Whether you've been arrested yourself, or you have seen it on TV when they read you your Miranda rights what do they say? "Anything you say will be used against you in evidence." There couldn't be more truth to that statement, anytime you speak and reveal information about yourself you give them power over you. Read this story.

In 1825, Nicolas I a new czar took the throne in Russia. The people were not happy about his position and a rebellion broke out. One of the leaders of the revolution, Kondraty Ryleyev was caught and sentenced to death. On the day of his execution he was lead up to the gallows and a noose was placed around his neck. The trapdoor fell and as Ryleyev hung the rope broke and he fell to the ground. During this era events like this were rare and when they did happen were seen as heavenly intervention and the person was pardoned. In this instance, Rylelyev stood to his feet and declared to the crowd, "Russia is such a stupid country, they can't do anything properly, even making a rope to hang a man is too difficult for them!"

A messenger went to the palace to deliver the news of the failed execution. Annoyed by this turn of events, as was customary, Nicolas went ahead and started to sign the pardon. Before his pen touched the paper, he asked, "Did Kondraty have anything to say after being saved from death? The messenger repeated what he had said and with that the Czar tore up the pardon and decided that he will prove him wrong and reissued the execution. The following day he was sent to the gallows again, and this time the execution was a success.

Once the words are released into the atmosphere you can't take them back. Therefore, keep a tight rein on them. Also refrain from using any type of sarcasm around your boss, as annoying as they might be you don't want to give them any ammunition to use against you.

Chapter 4: Reputation

The evil boss has a habit of tarnishing other people's reputation when things aren't going too well in his camp. The workaholic will say it's because his employees are lazy, the number cruncher will say someone submitted the wrong numbers……… and the list goes on. The bottom line is they want to keep their job and so will do anything in their power to ensure that any failure is blamed on someone else. You can make sure that person is never you by keeping your reputation spotless.

No matter how much you want to know every last detail about the people you are surrounded by it's just not possible. There is always something about them that you will never know about. If you were to think about this fact long enough it would make you paranoid; therefore, we choose to ignore this and judge people based on what we know about them, their words, gestures, actions, clothes and appearances. In any social setting, the yardstick that is used to make a judgment is based on appearance, and don't be fooled into believing anything else.

It is imperative that you create and maintain your own reputation, this gives you a certain degree of control over how you are judged by the people that you come into contact with and this is a powerful position to be in. This is a great way to start if you are the new kid on the block, if not don't worry you can still put these principles into practice.

Your reputation can either increase or decrease your strength; it can either repel or attract people. Whether your actions appear positive or negative all depends upon the reputation of the person who is performing them.

Initially, you are going to have to work to establish your reputation whether it is for generosity, honesty, or kindness, it is important that a positive characteristic is attached to your name. This quality will set you apart and position you in a league of your own, people will talk about you for this quality alone. Take the time to build your reputation with a firm foundation and it will spread like wildfire.

A strong reputation will always work for you so that you don't have to. It will cause you to have an aura that people respect and even fear. During World War II, a German general called Erwin Rommel had a reputation for deceptive and cunning maneuvering, everyone who met him was afraid of him. Even when he had lost all his soldiers and British tanks outnumbered German tanks by five to one, when news spread about his arrival, entire cities were evacuated because of his reputation.

As the saying goes, your reputation precedes itself, and before you have even arrived at your destination and spoken a single word your reputation has already spoken on your behalf.

Your evil boss won't know what to do with someone like you, in fact often times their only response will be to like you. If they have tried every trick in the book to get you to hang yourself and your feet are still firmly planted on the ground, they will start to respect you.

Chapter 5: Remain Positive

Your boss often sets the tone for the work environment, and if you have an evil manager......guess what? The atmosphere is going to be charged with negative energy and it's contagious. You will often find that when you have a bad boss there is all types of slandering and back biting going on. People hate coming to work, they are miserable and all this is brought into the office and this is what you are saturated in for 8 hours a day! You can't afford to allow your miserable manager to affect your attitude so keep your happy face on and stay positive no matter what you have to go through during the day.

Yes you are going to get irritated, angry, upset you may even shed a few tears. There is nothing wrong with experiencing these emotions just don't let them rule you. I once heard someone say that depression is like a tent, in other words its temporary! Don't build a house and live in your negative emotions.

It is human nature to see negative situations as something that we should avoid and we either bury our head in the sand and act like it doesn't exist or allow it to consume us. You can't afford to live like this, it will kill you. Unless your devil of a boss gets fired, they aren't going anywhere so you are going to have to deal with it! The first thing you should remember is that no situation is ever permanent, this too shall pass. You are not going to have to deal with this mess for the rest of your life. The second thing you should get into your spirit and allow to lead you in any unfair situation that you find yourself in is to change your perspective. Change the way you look at it. Listen to this interesting fact.

An eagle is the only bird in nature that doesn't fear storms, while all the other birds are running for cover; they use the storm to soar to the highest heights. This should be your mindset, use this negative situation to build yourself up spiritually. The only difference between the eagle and the rest of the birds is the way the eagle looks at the storm. You should see your negative situation as a building block instead of an obstacle.

Once upon a time, there was a king who decided to block the road with a massive boulder. He then hid and watched to see how people would react to the obstacle. The majority of people looked at the boulder in dismay but just walked around it and some blamed the king for allowing it to remain there. A few hours later, a peasant walked along the way with a great big bag of vegetables. The peasant decided to do what no one else had done; he put his bag down and pushed the boulder out of the way! It took him some time, but he managed to get the boulder out of the way. To his delight, he found a bag full of gold where the stone had been, in the bag was a note from the king saying that the whoever found the gold could keep it.

While everyone else saw the obstacle as a hindrance and walked around it, a simple change of mindset led to this man transitioning from peasant to prince in 2.5 seconds! It's amazing what can happen when we change our perspective on things. It is extremely important to remain positive and happy regardless of your situation your attitude will strengthen you and give you the drive you need to persevere in your circumstances. I am in no way saying that this is going to be easy, changing the way you think is difficult but it is possible.

Here are some tips to help you to remain positive when facing negative situations at work.

Gratitude

Gratitude is the key to remaining positive. You might not like your boss, but at least you have a job. While you are complaining about your manager there is someone struggling to feed their family and pay their bills and would love to put themselves in your shoes. When all hell is breaking loose in the workplace, if you are able to, sit at your desk and write down everything that you are grateful for. An attitude of gratitude will help you take your focus off the negative things that are going on around you and focus on the positive.

Control How You Feel

Your boss has no power over your emotions, you do. Eleanor Roosevelt once said, "no one can make you feel inferior without your consent." This is a very true statement, you might want to memorize it and meditate on it when you are having a bad day because of your boss. It can be difficult to realize this during a negative encounter but as you practice this it will start to become a habit. You have the power to choose how you feel and what you decide to focus on. No matter what your boss says or does, or how they try to make you feel, always keep this in the back of your mind, it is up to you to decide how you want to react to your situation.

Stay Away From Negative People

This is true in general, it is essential that we don't surround ourselves with negative people or they will suck the life out of us. Negative people are everywhere, at home, in the office, on the bus, you can't escape from them. The most important thing is that you don't allow their negativity to infect you, and the easiest way to do this is to stay away. Now, don't get me wrong, I'm not telling you to be rude and standoffish. Be polite, greet everyone with a smile. However, those lunchtime gossip meetings where everyone is talking about people behind their back, slandering the boss and whatever else is being said, keep away from that mess. It is easier to pull someone down from a table than it is for you to pull someone up onto a table. Negative people will drag you down to their level and even if you don't want to before you realize it you will be acting like them.

The funny thing about negative people is that they are often times right. When they are sitting down complaining about everything that is wrong they are looking at the situation for exactly what it is. You can't refute them when they are saying your boss is a miserable so and so because it's true. However, it's only a small mind that looks at a situation and sees it for what it is and isn't capable of seeing behind, over or around the issue. Think about it this way, is sitting down moaning and complaining at every opportunity going to change your situation? No, it isn't. All it will do is cause you to become a negative Nancy who sees the worst in everything. If you want to maintain a positive outlook in life you are going to have to stay away from the chronic complainers.

Decide to be positive

Remaining positive is a choice, you can either choose to be positive or you can choose to be negative! The decision is yours, thinking happy thoughts and focusing on good energy will ultimately make you feel better, and focusing on the negative is only going to make you feel terrible. You can avoid this and choose to be happy and positive.

A word of warning, misery loves company! Negative people have a tendency to hate positive people and they will do everything in their power to attempt to drag you down into their pit of despair. The forces of evil are going to come against you, it will be a battle, in fact you will find that people will start to throw daggers at you from all directions in attempts to burst your positive bubble. Persevere! Don't let anyone steal your joy. After a while you will find that the same negative people who were trying to lead you down a path of despair will want to know how to change their attitudes too. Joy is contagious, spread it like the plague, turn your office into a bundle of laughs and push out all that suffocating negative energy. The minions won't be able to beat you, the only choice they will have is to join you.

Chapter 6: Stress Relieving Methods

According to statistics the average professional is working on between 30 to 100 projects simultaneously! Modern workers are interrupted up to 7 times in an hour and spend 2 hours of the day being interrupted for issues that could be resolved outside of your help if the people were to just take a minute and think. Four out of 10 employees working for a large corporation are experiencing a major corporate restructuring which means that their futures are uncertain. So you have got all this to contend with as well as a hateful and evil boss! Life really isn't fair! This might be why 40% of working adults stay awake all night stressed out about the day's events and worrying about the day to come.

You are probably wondering how can I keep my focus when I have to deal with this tyrant? Is it even possible to do what needs to be done, take constant criticism from the devil and still have the energy left over to meet deadlines? How can I stop myself from going insane when I have all this on my plate? Harvard research have done some studies into stress management at work and have come up with some valuable stress relievers.

Act Instead of React

When we feel as if a situation is out of our control the stress hormone is activated and if this feeling remains constant it can erode concentration, confidence and our overall sense of well being. Harvard advises that you identify elements of the situation that you are capable of controlling and the ones that you can't. As previously stated, you are in control of how you react and respond to certain situations, but you can't control the way your boss decides to speak to you. Therefore, there are some things that you are just going to have to let slide.

Deep breathing

If you have just come out of a tense meeting with Dark Vader, or you are feeling overwhelmed and you need to get your head together take a time out! Find a quiet place and do some deep breathing exercises. Inhale for five seconds, hold your breath and exhale slowly through your nose. Do this repeatedly until you can feel the tension start to leave your body.

Eliminate Interruptions

The majority of us are bombarded throughout the day, whether its phone calls, emails, instant messages, deadlines, someone popping in the office, there is always some kind of interruption. You can't control how many times you are interrupted throughout the day but you can control how you respond to the interruption. You can either welcome it, shut it down, or evaluate how important it is and put it on your to do list. Often times an evil boss will bombard you with work that they are supposed to be doing. They will give you projects that are not on your job description which increases your workload. In such instances you need to speak up and let them know that this is not what you are paid to do. If necessary take it to higher management.

Take Regular Breaks

Contrary to popular belief, you won't get more done by working a 10 hour day without any breaks. When you try and do too much your productivity levels actually go down and your stress levels go up leaving you little energy to go home and enjoy your family. You don't want to get stuck in this type of rut so you should make a point of taking breaks several times throughout the day. I don't mean sit at your desk and stare at the computer screen; get up walk about stretch your legs. Energy Project pioneer Tony Schwartz states that if you have an intense 90 minute block of pure concentration and then have a break you can rejuvenate yourself and clear the stress build-up.

Healthy Eating and Rest

Staying up all night racking your brains about how you are going to deal with your evil boss the next day is a waste of time. Not getting enough sleep is only going to stress you out further and cause your productivity levels to drop. According to the Centers for Disease Control approximately 60 million Americans don't get enough sleep and this is an important recovery time for the body. If you are finding it difficult to sleep at night, experts recommend the following trick. Block your right nostril and breathe through your left for five minutes.

An unhealthy diet will stress your system out. It is advised that you consume a high protein low sugar diet. Cut out the carbs, the junk food and the sodas, it will make you feel lethargic and listless and when you are battling against an evil boss every day you need all the energy you can get.

Pressure Points

If you are the sort of person who panics when you are in a stressful situation there are several ways in which you can reduce your anxiety levels. One well known trick is to apply pressure to the side of your middle finger with your thumb, this will help to regulate your blood pressure and your stress levels will go down.

Humor

Now don't go and start laughing in your bosses face when they do something you don't like! That is NOT what I am telling you to do! However, humor is one of the most effective stress relievers. Laughter releases endorphins in the brain which instantly make you feel better.

Humor distracts you, it causes you to focus on the thing that you find funny instead of on the thing that is aggravating you and stressing you out. I don't know about you but there are certain things that make me laugh instantly like a comedy clip or watching one of my favorite comedians tell a joke. Whatever it is that makes you laugh have it to handy when you are at work. Keep laughing until you feel relaxed enough to face the music.

Chapter 7: Stay One Step Ahead of The Game

You have no control over how your evil boss chooses to behave. However, when your work life is organized and as far as you are aware things are running as smoothly as possible it makes it easier to cope when a tyrant is in the office. However, when things are all over the place and disorganized, when you are constantly running behind the last task that you forgot to accomplish, rushing to meet an urgent deadline or you are bouncing from one important task to the next life can become really difficult at work.

To stay one step ahead of the game, you need to plan your work day meticulously. Before you put your foot on the accelerator, you may need to put the brakes on so you can get organized. Organization is key to relieving a lot of stress in your life in general but it's also very effective in the workplace. Here are some tips to get you started.

Plan Your Day

You more or less know what work you need to get done in advance; every so often you might get a last minute project. Before you go to sleep at night organize your tasks for the following day.

Get a note pad and a pen and write down everything that you need to do the following day that includes emails, and phone calls. Once you have made your list, you will then need to prioritize them with the most important tasks being at the top of the list. When you have finished, put your notepad in your bag for the following day.

Meet Your Deadlines Early

Now I know this sounds unrealistic but it can be done. Meeting deadlines early will mean that you are going to have to make some sacrifices and one major one is to wake up early. Depending on your job it is more than likely that you will be able to complete a lot of your projects at home. Enjoy your evening, but instead of waking up at

7am wake up at 5am. It sounds like an impossible task but it will make your life a lot easier, a two hour head start gives you leverage and you can get a lot done in that time. If you can only work on your projects at work, go to work an hour early.

The trick is to make this a habit, instead of waking up early and getting on with work when you have a deadline to meet, do it every day. You will soon find that your days run a lot smoother because you are always one step ahead of the game.

Prepare For Your Meetings In Advance

Are you always the one who everyone has to wait for as you flick through your notes as you try and make your point? Well it's time for that to come to an end. You should always keep this in mind, what you and your colleagues get out of a meeting is dependent upon what you put into a meeting through preparation. You never get what you need when you are not prepared. Here are some things you can do to prepare for a meeting:

1. **Set An Agenda:** A meeting without an agenda is a waste of time, set an agenda and distribute it to your colleagues at least three days prior to the meeting so that everyone is on the same page and knows what topic will be addressed during the meeting.
2. **Review Materials:** You don't want your meeting to become a reading session. When you wait until the day of the meeting to provide reading material your attendees are left with no choice but to read them during the meeting. Make sure you send all review materials out at least three days before the meeting.
3. **Set the Expectations:** An agenda is different to the expectations. You need to let your team know what you hope to achieve from the meeting. You need to be descriptive with the subject and call the

meeting something like, "a brief on the status of project ABC." This will lead to a more productive meeting.

Through careful planning you won't have to live your work life battling against the next deadline every day. You will definitely have one battle, that of the evil boss! But that battle won't seem so stressful when you've won the war against everything else.

Chapter 8: See the Bigger Picture

For those of you who have a vision greater than working for a tyrant boss for the rest of your life I applaud you! For those who don't, I suggest you get one. The bigger picture is that you have a plan and a vision that extends outside of your current work situation. You have a set goal that you are working towards and that is what you need to keep focused on. If you have a dream that has died, I suggest that you call it from the grave and resurrect it right now, breathe into it and give it life. Your vision is something that you need to keep focused on or it will get lost in the weeds that you are subject to on a daily basis at work.

I am just throwing out numbers here, so let's say you have a goal to have your own business up and running within 3 years, you can go into work every day with a smile on your face knowing that you are one step closer to your destiny. When your focus is on your circumstances and not on your vision, it's easy to get depressed and bitter when you have to deal with an evil boss. So what can you do to keep your dream alive and ensure that you achieve it by the deadline you have set for yourself so you don't have to stay in a job that you hate until you retire?

Write Your Vision Down

I am certain that you have heard more than once how important it is to set goals for yourself. Unfortunately, the majority of us don't have clear measurable goals to work towards. According to a study conducted among students at a Dominican University, people who wrote their goals down accomplished significantly more than those who didn't. I am sure you want to accomplish more than the average, if this is true then get a pen and paper out and write your goals down.

Your dream is no good in your head, you can think about it all day long but if you don't have a clear road map of how you are going to get there, there is a high probability that you won't get there. Once you have written it down, don't leave it sitting in your notepad, pin it somewhere you can see it every day and read it out loud daily. This is how you give your vision life. Write out multiple copies and leave it in places that you know you have to visit on a daily basis. Leave it on your desk at work; stick it on your dressing mirror, on your bathroom mirror. It is important that your vision is kept before your eyes so that you don't forget.

Make it Measurable

So you have a goal, great! That's fantastic; the main question is how are you going to get there. You need to create a timeframe and a specific plan of action. If you want to own your own company you may need to take some courses in business management. Whatever your goals are, find out what you need to do to achieve them and get on with it.

Create Benchmarks

When you are looking at the end result of your vision, it can look impossible. When you have broken it down into small actionable steps, the goal becomes much more realistic. So now that you have a plan of action, work out how long it will take to achieve each phase of your goal and stick to it. When you have a benchmark, you can measure your progress. If you find that you are moving more slowly than expected, make adjustments.

Celebrate Your Success

The most important aspect of setting goals is celebrating your success. The main aim of setting goals is achieving them, and once you hit each benchmark you can celebrate your success. Celebrating every small victory will motivate you to continue working towards the main vision.

Now that you have your plan of action stick to it! And remind yourself where you are headed every time your evil boss starts acting up.

Chapter 9: Remain Immune To Your Bosses Behavior

An evil boss can act bipolar a lot of the time. One minute they are up, bragging about the achievements of their team; the next minute they are down screaming at everyone because a project hasn't been completed. I am in no way trying to justify this behavior, it's wrong and there is no excuse for it. However, when you are in a high powered position, stress levels are going to be high and mood swings can be expected. There are also some bosses who just switch on and off randomly for no apparent reason. One minute they are the best person to be around and the next they are just evil! And of course anyone who is in the line of fire gets hit, including you!

Regardless of the mood of your boss your work has to get done. So how can you keep your bosses mood swings from affecting your moods and your productivity? This isn't going to be an easy task, but it can be done. Here are some steps to get you started.

Ignore It

When your evil boss is walking the floor sounding off about how useless the team is because a deadline was missed or targets are not being met and the team isn't moving fast enough, bla bla bla. It's likely that everyone else will take on this mindset, when the boss is in a good mood so is everyone else. When the boss is in a bad mood, so is everyone else!

It is important to understand that you don't have to follow the trend because it's really easy to do. Firstly negative energy is contagious, and second of all most people don't like to go against the status quo so they will follow along with the dominant theme. You can resist this by keeping things in perspective, why is your boss in a bad mood? If it is because a project wasn't finished on time and you weren't working on that project then don't let it bother you, it has nothing to do with your performance. If you are a part of the project, let your manager know that you are on track with your assigned task.

The majority of the time our priorities and assignments are not the same as our managers, so there is no need for what they are going through to have any effect on you.

Look For Triggers

Pay attention to the temper tantrums of your boss and see if you notice a pattern. Often times you will find that there are certain things in particular that trigger their bad moods. For example, does your boss get irritated in the morning before the weekly executive report is due? Or after lunch on Wednesday when they have to leave at 4pm on the dot to get to their sons soccer match? Or maybe it's a routine that takes place every day that starts as soon as they enter the building until they have had their 5th cup of coffee?

Whatever the reason, you can identify the triggers that cause your boss to direct their emotions to everyone in ear shot. Once you know what they are, you can work around the moods, stay away when the storm is brewing and get what you need when the storm has passed.

Avoidance Tactics

This is especially true when you know all hell is about to break loose, but it's also a good idea to keep your distance in general. Sometimes this is not always going to be possible, you might have an urgent question that has to be answered, or you might have an important meeting scheduled. But if you don't and it's not urgent, it's ok to email a question instead of spending half an hour trying to pluck up the courage to go into their office.

Avoidance may not work all the time, your boss might decide to pull a drive by and stop off at your desk for some face to face interaction. If that's the case, you are just going to have to roll with the punches.

Don't Take it Personally

Too often employees take their bosses negative comments to heart. Please don't do this. First I want you to remember this, and I think this is more important than anything. Even though your boss might act like an animal, he or she is a human being with emotions and feelings. Often times when people are angry and bitter they don't intend on being that way, life gets to them and they don't know how else to handle it. You have no idea what they have to go through at home or in any other aspect of their personal lives for that matter. If it's a woman she may get abused by her partner, she may have found out that her partner is having an affair. There are so many things that could be wrong in their life. There could be other issues affecting their behavior, whatever the reason, don't assume that it has anything to do with you because nine times out of ten it won't.

Address the Situation Calmly

If your boss is really just too much, you may want to make an attempt at approaching them.

Tread very carefully here and remain as calm as you possibly can. There is a scripture in the bible that says a harsh word stirs up anger and a soft word turns away wrath. (Proverbs 15:1) As annoying as your boss may be, keep your tone as neutral as possible and refrain from displaying a hint of anger. If their outburst is due to a project, you may want to offer your time to help get things moving. A kind gesture will always turn a positive situation around.

Chapter 10: Improve Your Communication Skills

Whether or not you think you have great communication skills or not is irrelevant, you can always improve. Even though your boss found themselves in management its quite obvious from the way he/she speaks to people that they are lacking effective communication skills. What's that got to do with me? I hear you asking, it has nothing to do with you but the better you are at dealing with people the easier it will become for you to handle your tyrannical boss.

Research has concluded that one of the most fundamental skills required to succeed in the workplace is good communication skills. When you evaluate the world's greatest leaders, what you will find is that they all had excellent communication skills so it only makes sense that you brush up on yours. Here are some tips to help you.

Learn How to Listen

Have you ever wanted to have an important conversation with someone and you couldn't get a word in edgeways? I am sure you have experienced it. It is really important that you listen to what the other person has to say before you formulate your response. To avoid any misunderstanding, ask for clarification. Whoever is speaking to you should be the most important person in the world and they should have your undivided attention. It doesn't matter whether you are face to face or on the phone, people can detect when you are truly listening or not. If you are on the phone, don't hold the phone between your ear and your shoulder at the same time as loudly tapping out an email. You might miss something important and often times when that happens the person won't say it again because they have sensed that you really aren't interested in what they are saying.

Use Appropriate Language

No matter how friendly you are with senior management; when you are communicating with them make sure you use formal language. When you are sending an email or a text message speak in full, correct sentences so that you are not misunderstood. An effective communicator will structure their message based on who they are speaking to so always keep the other person in mind when you are sending a message.

Body Language

One thing you don't want to do is give your boss any clues that you don't like him/her. Yes it may be true that you can't stand them but that doesn't mean they have to know about it. Unfortunately, actions speak louder than words and this applies to your body language. You might be saying one thing with your mouth but your body is screaming something else and that's what the person hears. When you are speaking to your boss don't cross your arms in front of you, this is an indication that you are not open for conversation, and that you have put a barrier across yourself for protection. When you don't make eye contact it is generally an indication that you are trying to hide something, and in your case it's that you don't like your boss.

Be Specific but Brief

Long winded chatter is annoying in general, but when you are in a business setting and time is of the essence it is even more so. During verbal and written communication practice brevity and at the same time be specific. You want to provide enough information to get your point across so that the other person understands what you are trying to say. If your response is to an email, make sure that you read the entire email before responding, this will ensure that your reply is appropriate.

Write it Down

Whether you are in a one on one meeting or a team meeting, make sure that you write down everything that is said. Don't try and memorize everything because more than likely you are going to forget. If you had a one to one meeting, send your manager an email detailing what was discussed and any resolutions that you came to.

Think Before You Speak

Last but not least, think about what you are about to say before you say it. Always bear in mind that you can't take anything back once it has been released. The smart thing to do is not say it in the first place. This especially applies when you are around your evil boss. Even though they are probably just hateful and vengeful anyway, you don't want to give him or her an excuse to really not like you.

Chapter 11: Improve Your Conflict Resolution Skills

When dealing with an evil boss you are going to have continuous conflict and you may as well get used it! Instead of allowing it to bother you improve your conflict resolution skills so that you are ready when the battle arises.

Regardless of how healthy your relationships are a certain level of conflict is actually normal. Everyone has their own individual personalities and people are not always going to agree on things. Learning how to handle conflict instead of avoiding it is important. Mismanaged conflict will damage a relationship, but when handled in a positive and respectful way conflict can strengthen the bond that you have with that person (this is speaking in general by the way, I am well aware that you don't want to strengthen your bond with your evil boss) By learning how to deal with conflict effectively, you will continue to maintain strong and healthy relationships.

The Reasons for Conflict

In most cases, conflict is a result of a difference in opinion, it occurs when people disagree over their motivations, values, perceptions, desires or ideas. Sometimes these differences don't seem important, but when a conflict triggers strong emotions, a deep personal need is often at the root of the problem. The deeper problem could be the need to feel valued and respected, the need to feel secure and safe, or the need for greater intimacy and closeness.

Everyone needs to feel supported, understood and nurtured, but how these needs are met differ greatly. A difference in the need to feel safe and comfortable create some of the most difficult conflicts in our professional and personal relationships. Evaluate the conflicting need for continuity and safety, verses the need to take risks and explore. This conflict often takes place between parents and toddlers. The need of the child is to explore, so the hilltop or the road meets a need. But the need of the parent is to protect the child and keep them from harm and danger. The parents need is seen as limiting the toddler's exploration which becomes a conflict between the two.

The needs of every individual play an important role in the long term success of the majority of relationships. Each person's needs deserves consideration and respect. In personal relationships when one party feels that their needs are not being met, it results in arguments, distance and inevitably a break up. In the workplace, a difference in needs is often at the main cause of bitter disputes which can lead to lost jobs, a loss in profit and broken deals. When you are able to recognize that everyone's needs are important no matter how trivial they appear to us, and you are open to examining them in a understanding and compassionate environment, it opens the door to team building, creative problem solving and improved relationships.

What is Your Perception of Conflict?

Are you afraid of conflict? Do you go to great lengths to avoid it? If the way you view conflict comes from painful or frightening memories from early childhood or previous unhealthy relationships, there is a possibility that you have a fear that there will be a negative ending to all disagreements. You might see conflict in a relationship as humiliating, demoralizing, dangerous and fearful. If any of your life experiences have left you feeling powerless and out of control, there is a possibility that conflict is traumatic to you.

If you see conflict as being dangerous, when conflict arises you will automatically feel threatened making it difficult to handle the problem at hand in a healthy way. Instead, you might have an angry outburst or shut down completely.

Unhealthy responses to conflict

- Incapable of recognizing and responding appropriately to things that are important to the other person.
- Angry and violent outbursts.
- Withholding love resulting in isolation, rejection, shame and fear of abandonment.
- Incapable of compromising and seeing things from the other person's point of view.
- Fearing and avoiding conflict as well as expecting a negative outcome.

Healthy Responses to Conflict

- The ability to recognize and respond appropriately to things that matter to the other person.
- Non-defensive and calm reactions.
- Willing to forget, forgive and move on without holding anger or resentment towards the other person.

- The ability to compromise without administering vengeful punishment.
- Believing that it is better to resolve conflict than to avoid it.

Conflict Resolution Stress and Emotions

Conflict invites strong emotions and can lead to disappointment, hurt feelings and discomfort. When conflict is not handled the right way it can cause resentments, breakups, stress and tension. When conflict is dealt with in a healthy way it builds trust, strengthens relationships and enables us to understand people better. Your ability to resolve conflicts successfully depends on the following:

- **Handle stress efficiently at the same time as remaining calm and alert.** When you remain calm in a conflict situation, you are better able to interpret and read nonverbal and verbal communication.

- **Remain in control of your behavior and emotions:** When your emotions are under control, you are better able to articulate your needs without frightening or threatening others.
- **Pay attention to how you are expressing your feelings:** Even though you might be upset, don't express yourself in a way that belittles or threatens others.
- **Respect other people's differences:** A difference in opinion does not make the other person wrong. Refrain from patronizing beliefs and ideas when you are trying to get your point across.

To resolve conflict efficiently and effectively, there are two core skills you will need to practice and learn: the ability to reduce stress levels as soon as there is any sign of conflict. The ability to control your emotions and perform effectively even while in the midst of a disagreement.

1. **Efficiently Reduce Stress**

The key to remaining balanced is having the ability to relieve stress in the middle of a conflict. It is essential that you are capable of remaining in control and focused regardless of the challenges you are facing. If you don't know how to remain grounded and in control of your emotions, conflict will overwhelm you and you will be unable to respond in a healthy way.

American psychologist Connie Lillas describes the way people typically respond when they are overwhelmed by stress using a driving analogy:

- **Foot on the accelerator:** A stress response when irritated and angry is the inability to sit still.
- **Foot on the brake:** A response when you are withdrawn or depressed is to show little emotion or energy, to shut the world out.
- **Foot on the accelerator and the brake:** On the surface it

appears as if there is nothing wrong because you are not reacting. However, this is simply because you have become immobilized by what has happened. Underneath the exterior, you are really angry and ready to explode.

Stress stops you from being able to handle conflict by preventing you from:

- Accurately reading nonverbal communication.
- Listen to what the other person is trying to say.
- Being in touch with your own feelings.
- Understanding what your needs are.
- Articulating your needs in a way that others will be able to understand.

Do you suffer from stress?

Stress may be so normal to you that you don't realize that you are stressed. If you identify with the following traits, you might have a problem with stress in your life.

- You often have the feeling of tightness or tensity in certain parts of your body.
- When you breathe, you are unaware of the movement that is taking place in your chest or stomach.
- The majority of your time is spent dealing with conflict.

Emotional Awareness

To understand yourself and others, you need to be emotionally aware. If you can't understand how you are feeling or why you are feeling this way, you won't be able to resolve disagreements because you are unable to articulate your feelings effectively.

It may sound simple to understand your own feelings, but many people don't want to deal with what they are feeling and so they ignore it. In order to handle conflict, you must be connected to your feelings and emotions. If you shy away from strong emotions, or your focus is on solutions that are purely rational, you will be limited in your ability to face and resolve conflict.

Emotional awareness is being conscious of your feelings at any given moment. Being able to handle your feelings in a healthy way is the foundation of the communication process responsible for conflict resolution.

Emotional awareness helps you to:

- Understand what other people are dealing with.
- Understand what you are dealing with.
- Remain motivated while the conflict is being resolved.
- Communicate openly and effectively
- Influence and attract others

Conflict Resolution and non verbal communication

The things that people don't say often says more than what they do say. Nonverbal communication is often displayed through posture, facial expressions, pace, gesture, intensity and tone of voice.

It is important to listen to what is felt as well as what is said in a conflict situation. The ability to listen in this way informs us, strengthens us and in turn makes it easier for others to understand us.

When you are in the middle of a conflict, paying attention to nonverbal signs will help you to understand what other people are really trying to say. This gives you the ability to make the appropriate response in a way that will build trust so that the other person opens up and speaks openly about what the real problem actually is. A reassuring touch, a calm tone of voice, or a concerned and interested facial expression can reduce tension during a conflict.

Your ability to read another person accurately is dependent upon your emotional awareness. The more in-tune you are with your own emotions, the easier you will be able to discern what others are saying through nonverbal signals.

Tips for resolving and managing conflict

Resolving and managing conflict effectively requires that you have the ability to reduce stress levels efficiently and bring your emotions under control. A conflict can be resolved quickly and end on a positive note if you comply with the following guidelines:

- **Listen to feelings not just what is said:** When you can accurately interpret what others are really saying by listening to their emotional needs through what they don't say, you build trust. This makes it easier for the other person to listen to you when it is your turn to speak.
- **Make resolving the conflict the priority instead of winning:** There are times when you are simply going to have to agree to disagree which means

compromise. This is the easiest way to resolve a resolution, people are more willing to go half way than to have their needs completely disregarded.

- **Focus on what is going on in that moment:** Being angry about what happened last week and bringing that into what happened today is only going to raise tension further. Focus on what is going on in the present and do your best to ensure that it is resolved effectively.

- **Choose your battles wisely:** Don't waste time arguing over trivial issues. Conflict resolution is emotionally draining and if your time is spent dealing with every little thing that goes wrong you will get tired very quickly. Think about it this way, if you have been driving around a car park for 15 minutes looking for a space and one comes up you are going to want to grab it as quickly as possible and you won't want to give it up. However, if there are plenty of other spots why fight over the one that someone beat you to when you can just go and find another one?

- **Forgiveness:** If you are not willing to forgive the other party for an offense, conflict resolution is going to be very difficult. Being able to resolve conflict lies in our ability to release the offender without the desire for revenge. Holding on to anger is emotionally draining, let it go!

Resolve conflict using humor

Once emotion and stress are brought into an even keel it allows you to release pleasure, joy and playfulness. Joy is a very powerful; studies have shown that you can overcome adversity as long as you remain joyful through it. When dealing with conflict, humor can play the same role.

You can resolve disagreements and arguments, and avoid confrontations by using humor to communicate your thoughts. Humor takes the edge off things, and makes it easier to say things that would otherwise be difficult to communicate. However, it is important that the other person does not feel as if you are laughing at them but with them. When humor is used to resolve conflict, it can be used as a time to build a stronger relationship.

Chapter 12: How to cope when your boss is a bully

A boss who bullies his employees is a completely different breed to the one who is just challenging or annoying. Dealing with such an employer can be an isolating and depressing experience. This type of boss is unfortunately quite common. According to a CIPD study, 91% of employees believe that their company does not take workplace bullying seriously.

If you don't want to leave your job, but you have a boss who is making your life at work difficult there are several things that you can do to handle the issue.

Confide in a mentor or a neutral third party

Depending on the type of company that you work for, you were probably assigned a mentor. A mentor helps you to settle into your new role and they are someone you can talk to who is outside of your team if you are experiencing any problems. When you discuss your issues with them, you may find that they have been through a similar experience and they can give you practical survival tips or point you in the right direction to someone who can help.

A mentor or a neutral third party may be able to intervene on your behalf. It is important that the person who you confide in is impartial to ensure that there is no bias involved when dealing with the situation.

Speak to your boss

This might sound like an impossible task especially after a heated discussion, or you may feel too intimidated. However, some people are so set in their ways and are not aware that their behavior is imposing or threatening. By confronting the person in a non judgmental way, you may open their eyes to how their demeanor is affecting others.

Have an open and honest discussion, and explain to your boss that the way they treat you is having a negative impact on your life. You may find that speaking up improves your situation. Research conducted by Ohio State University discovered that employees who defended themselves against their manager where less psychologically disturbed than those who didn't.

However, if you choose to walk through this door, prepare yourself. Since your manager is not going to be prepared for what you are going to say, come armed with solutions instead of just bringing the problems.

Speak to human resources

If the above options fail, you may need to speak to your human resources department and file a formal complaint against your boss. This should be the last resort if you are really suffering and the situation has become unbearable. Approaching HR may feel slightly overwhelming; however, unless you plan on remaining under the foot of your tyrant boss, this is something you will have to do. It formalizes what you have already said to your manager and may even scare them into changing their behavior. You should also remember that there is a high chance that you are not the only person who is being bullied but they are afraid to come forward. You will often find that when one person speaks out others do too.

By taking a proactive approach to defend yourself you are behaving professionally and taking the appropriate steps to resolve an issue that is also affecting others. Tension results in an unproductive workforce so it is in everyone's best interest to get the issue resolved.

Don't allow it to affect your self esteem

When someone is constantly criticizing you it can have a negative effect on how you see yourself. It may cause you to question whether you are adding value to the company and make you feel as if you are not important to them. Periodically take the time out to go over positive feedback from other colleagues or clients and look back on projects where your contribution caused it to be a success. This will help you to remember why you got the job to begin with and why it's important to you. The bottom line is this; if you know in your heart that you are doing the best that you can do, don't allow another person's expectations define how you see yourself.

A company employee spends the majority of their time at work; therefore it is important that you feel valued and happy. When you spend the weekends not looking forward to Monday's, it makes it difficult to enjoy your time off. Although a challenging boss is completely different to a bully, both can be resolved by speaking up and trying to manage the situation in a constructive and professional way. If it means that you will start feeling positive about your job again and enjoy coming to work, it will be worth it.

Chapter 13: How to motivate yourself in the workplace

Regardless of whether or not you have an evil boss, to succeed in the workplace you need to function at a high level and you can only do so if you are at your best. When you don't need anyone to inspire you and you are driven from within everything else will fall into place. Here are some ways to motivate yourself in the workplace.

Start as you mean to go on

Rolling out of bed every morning an hour before you need to be at work is not going to do you any good. Rushing around so trying to make sure you are not late creates stress that you don't need. If you start your day well, the rest of your day is likely to follow suit. The first habit that you need to practice is to wake up early, this gives you the chance to mentally prepare for the day ahead. You need to psyche yourself up and go over everything that you need to do that day and remind yourself that you are more than capable of completing the tasks that you have set for yourself.

Put a dollar on it

It shouldn't come as much of a surprise to you that money is a great way to motivate yourself. However, after you have worked at the same job for a while it is easy to forget why we do what we do. Remind yourself of how much you get paid for your contribution and that your salary will help you to fulfill your goals. Whether it's to buy a new home, a new car or to go on vacation, never lose sight of the reason why you have to work. Regardless of whether you are on a salaried income, or your pay is dependent upon how hard you work you should always put your best efforts forward.

Focus on personal growth and development

Whatever your position is at present, there is always room for improvement. There may be a promotion at work that you can prepare yourself for or the opportunity to move to another branch. This can be another motivating factor to keep you working hard. You should work as if your superiors are always watching you and looking for someone to promote, and even if this is not said in public, this is typically the case. Management is always looking for new leadership. Keeping your focus on your potential career growth should always be a motivating factor in why you choose to do your best. Your evil boss may not be giving you the recognition that you deserve but there is a high possibility that someone else is watching you and will put your name forward when there is a promotion.

Stay positive

In a recent survey about the advantages of working from home, one of the main benefits chosen was being away from negativity. When you have a bad boss, or things are not going well with the company, people have a tendency to constantly focus on the negative. When you are surrounded by constant bickering, even if you are not involved, it will have an effect on your subconscious mind. It can then become extremely difficult to remain motivated when negativity is all you are hearing. No matter what work environment you are in, there is good and bad in every office. Surround yourself with the positive people in the office who are of the same mindset as you and you can motivate each other.

Healthy competition

If you work in a performance driven environment such as sales, you can indulge in healthy competition where you all strive to be the best sales person. This can defiantly motivate you to push yourself because at the end of the day, everyone loves to win. Even if you don't work in a sales environment you should always strive to be better than your work colleagues. Not in a narcissistic way but simply as a way of bettering yourself. Things such as being the first to resolve an issue, being more professional or the first person to answer a question. These are all ways in which you can secretly compete with your peers and motivate yourself to do better. Competition is a healthy way of pushing yourself to grow.

Your own personal accomplishments

You should want to return home after a hard day's work and be proud of what you have done. You are at work at a minimum of 8 hours per day; this is a clear indication that it is an important part of your life. Whatever job you do, treat it with pride and your motivation levels will soar like an eagle. I once remember passing by a street cleaner, and he was having the time of his life. Singing and laughing, striking up conversation with people who walked by at the same time as doing a fantastic job. You should approach your job with the same attitude. Even if you are not yet working in your ideal job, you are there for a reason so focus on that reason and make it a pleasant and joyful experience, because being miserable is no fun, you can ask your evil boss about that! When you go to bed at night instead of thinking about how much you dread going into work the next morning, think about what you have accomplished for the day and pat yourself on the back for a job well done and have a comfortable night's sleep knowing that you did your best today and you will continue to do your best tomorrow.

Chapter 14: Don't Outshine Your Boss

In the first year of King Louis XIV's reign he had a finance minister named Nicolas Fouquet. He was a giving person who loved grandiose parties, poetry and beautiful women. He also had a preference for the high life and loved money, his life was extravagant to say the least. When the Prime Minister died, Fouquet was expecting to replace him. However, the King had previously decided that the position was no longer necessary. This and several other indications made Fouquet insecure and led him to feel as if he was no longer in good standing with the king. To impress the king and win back his affection Fouquet decided to throw the most lavish party that the world had ever seen. He claimed that the purpose of the party was to celebrate the completion of his chateau, but the real reason was to try and impress the king who he crowned the guest of honor.

Some of the most well known people in Europe at the time were invited to the party. A moving play was performed; there was a sophisticated seven course dinner with oriental food that had not yet been experienced in Europe. The guests dined to music played by some of the most skilled musicians in the country, all in honor of the king.

After dinner the guests were led through the chateau's gardens, Fouquet personally escorted the king. When they arrived at the canals they were greeted by a marvelous display of fireworks. The party continued into the late night hours and everyone agreed that it was the most spectacular affair they have ever attended.

The following day Fouquet was arrested by the king's head musketeer. He later went on trial for stealing money from the treasury when in actual fact all that he was accused of was done with the king's permission. Fouquet was sentenced to a prison in France; he spent the last twenty years of his life in isolation.

King Louis XIV was a very arrogant and proud man, who had to be at the center of attention continuously. He could not stand to be overshadowed by anyone, and especially not by someone who he considered to be his superior. To succeed Fouquet, Louis selected Jean-Baptiste Colbert, a man renowned for his stinginess and for holding the most boring parties in Paris. Colbert made certain that all money that came from the treasury was handed directly to the King. Louis XIV used this money to build a palace more extravagant than Fouquet's, known today as the palace of Versailles and also hosted parties that were more lavish than his.

Let us look at why Fouquet ended up on the bad side of the King. During his party, he presented event after event to the king, with each one being more spectacular than the other. He thought that what he was doing would impress the king and get him back into his good books. He assumed that showing off his good taste and his high connections would impress the king demonstrating that he would make the best prime minister. Instead, everything that he did backfired! With every gasp of awe, every smile, every word of gratitude and congratulations directed towards Fouquet, the king got more and more angry. Fouquet and the king saw this event through completely different eyes. The king believed that he was showing off and intentionally trying to outshine him. Since many of the king's friends were present at the party, the mere fact that they were impressed by the spectacle caused the king to believe that his own friends were now more in awe of Fouquet than they were of him, and this he wasn't going to tolerate. King Louis XIV was in fact offended and not flattered by the event, of course he was not going to admit this to anyone, but instead made a convenient excuse to get rid of the man who made him feel insecure.

This is typically the fate of anyone who challenges his master's vanity or sense of self worth whether it is done intentionally or not.

You can be the most beautiful, talented, richest person in the world but still have insecurities. This is normal, and everyone has them, the down side of this is when you are talented or gifted in a certain area, you are going to stir up all kinds of envy, resentment and manifestations of insecurity. This is something you should expect and do not waste time worrying about people's inabilities to be content with who they are. However, when it comes to those who have been placed in a position of authority over you, a different approach is required. Do not delude yourself into thinking anything has changed since the days of Louis XIV, human nature does not change. People who are at the top of their game are seen as kings and queens by those beneath them. They want to feel secure in their position, and superior to those around them in wit, intelligence and charm.

I am hoping you have connected the dots by now, if not let me explain. Your boss is evil because of insecurity and this applies to all evil bosses regardless of the category they are in. Regardless of whether you like them or not, they are in a management position because they worked to get there and they are proud of their accomplishments. They also see their subordinates as inferior to them hence the disrespectful treatment of their employees and everything else that comes with those who are on a power trip. The minute they feel threatened by you, they will start planning your demise. You may not mean to outshine your boss, it's just your nature, your personality is attractive and you stand out in a crowd. Even though you can't help it, and it's not something you are doing intentionally, you may need to tone it down a bit when you are in front of your boss.

If you are one of your boss's favorites, don't get too comfortable in your position. Let me illustrate what I am trying to say. In Japan, during the late sixteenth century, Sen no Rikyu was the favorite of Emperor Hideyoshi; he was his most trusted advisor, honored throughout the country and had his own apartment in the palace. Despite all this, Hideoyshi had the police arrest him and sentenced him to death. Instead of dying from execution, Rikyu chose to commit suicide instead. What was the reason for this sudden turn of events, you would assume that he committed some atrocity. Rikyu was once a peasant and ascended from peasantry to the emperor's favorite. He was so excited about his new position that he made a wooden statue with sandals on his feet. (the sandals are a sign of nobility) He then went and positioned the statue in the most important temple in the palace, in a location where it was seen by everyone who walked by.

To Hideyoshi this was a sign that Rikyu had no sense of boundaries and that he thought he was on the same level as the rest of the nobility when in fact he was seen as nothing but a lucky peasant. How dare he get too big for his boots! Rikyu got too excited about his position and actually started to see himself as an equal, he paid for this gross misrepresentation with his life.

Remember the following, don't ever take your position as favorite for granted, and don't allow any favors you receive go to your head. As you have read, one wrong move and you are out! Now that you know the dangers that are associated with outshining your boss, you can turn this to your advantage. First you must puff up and flatter your evil boss, (I can already see you cringing)! I don't mean that you go around singing your bosses praises, do it very discreetly so he/she is aware of it but no one else is. Even if you don't feel as if they deserve any type of flattery this is simply a survival mechanism that works. For example, you might know that you are more intelligent than your boss and should be in their position, don't act like this is what you think by flaunting your intellect. Act naive and always make them feel as if they are indeed much more intelligent than you. Ask for help even if you don't need it because this will make your boss feel as if you need their expert advice.

If you come up with a grandiose idea that increased the bottom line of the company, when it comes to public meetings about how well this idea has benefited the organization, instead of taking the credit, use this opportunity to tell the board that you would not have come up with the idea if it wasn't for the superior advice of your manager.

If you have a more witty personality than your manager, tone down your humor and don't make he/she appear cold or glum in comparison and always look for ways that you can make them seem more charismatic and cheerful. If you are a social butterfly, don't be the cloud that overshadows the radiance of your boss. He/she must appear like the sun, the center of attention which everyone revolves around radiating brilliance and power. If you are placed in a position where you have to entertain your boss, learn from the mistake of Fouquet and don't put on a show that's too grandiose, it could backfire.

I am in no way advocating that you should downplay your natural gifted abilities in every setting. You can decide when to use this advice and when not to, you can't live your life walking on eggshells concerned about who you are upsetting because of your gifts. However, when dealing with an evil boss, this strategy is one of your best weapons.

Chapter 15: If All Else Fails, Kill Them With Kindness

"Kill them with kindness" is not just a cheesy quote on a motivational poster; this message when put into practice can make your life a whole lot easier when working with an evil boss. Instead of stooping to their level and engaging in a battle kill your manager with kindness which will not only knock him/her off their high horse but you will score brownie points with your co-workers for your superior people skills and your ability to deal with difficult people because the entire office knows how hard it is to work with your manager, they have to deal with their nonsense on a daily basis too!

What if we took a step back and decided to respond to cruelty with kindness? You may think that being kind to someone when they are being mean to you is a sign of weakness, but in actual fact it actually empowers you. It takes willpower, a strong mind and patience to display kindness in the face of cruelty. There are several reasons why you should take steps in this direction.

It prevents arguments and could turn your enemy into a friend

Kindness is a very powerful resource that has been grossly underestimated. Being kind to someone who has wronged you may cause them to have second thoughts about continuing on in a battle with you. It can prick their conscience so that they stop their hate campaign against you.

It can be very tempting to just engage in a battle with someone, at the beginning it can be very satisfying; however, it will only drain your energy in the long run. Kindness is contagious and enables you to be more tolerant of people in general no matter how rude and disrespectful they may be.

It allows you to be proactive instead of reactive

By responding to your enemies with kindness, it lets them know that they don't have any power over you. They expect you to respond in the same way that they do and when you don't, it shocks them and sends a strong statement that you will not allow people to dictate how you react or how you feel, and that you choose what actions you choose to display and not them.

It is a sign of victory

Some people are rude and unkind because they know that they can't beat you and it's frustrating to them knowing that you are so strong and they are so weak. As they throw dagger after dagger in your back but you don't appear to flinch it starts to become very clear that they can't move you and that there is something about your character that is impenetratable because they know that if it was them, they would have broken both your legs by now. Without them even realizing it, they wave the white flag of surrender and give up on their vendetta against you.

You reap what you sow

No matter how evil your boss is, you should never seek revenge. That sounds really difficult but when you look at it from the following perspective, this rule becomes a lot easier to follow. Whatever you put into the world through word action or deed, the world gives it right back to you ten times over. Think about it like this, a farmer sows a single seed into the ground and waits for a return. He gets back much more than his original seed, one apple seed reaps an entire apple tree! The same law applies to your decision to do good or bad when a person offends you. Once that person releases their evil into the atmosphere, by law it is going to come back to them. You may not see the manifestation of it before your eyes, but trust and do believe that one day they will reap the evil that they sent into the world. If you then turn around and do something equally as evil to get revenge on them, it might feel good temporarily to watch them squirm, but it will only be a matter of time before that act of evil comes back to you. Therefore, it is imperative that no matter how evil your boss is, you do not seek any type of revenge because in the end it will come back to you worse than how you originally administered it.

Now that we know why you should kill your boss with kindness, let's look at how to do this. Please bear in mind that this is not about being manipulative and secretly spiteful. If you are genuine about your kindness, you will find that you will be rewarded at the end of the battle.

Don't fight fire with fire

Dealing with an evil boss can be emotionally draining. Whether your boss is new or you have been dealing with them for a long period of time it's really easy to snap and be as rude to them as they are being to you. When you feel as if you can't keep your head above water and you feel as if you are going to take a trip down the road of no return take a deep breath, smile and remember that you are the bigger person.

Be genuine

This can be difficult, how can you be genuinely kind to someone who is genuinely rude? Have you heard the term "fake it until you make it," this is what you are going to have to do. Although your blood may be boiling it makes it easier to be genuinely kind to your evil boss because at the end of the day, you know that you are in the right and you are simply dealing with a difficult person, this in itself will help you to be nice when you really don't want to.

Who would you rather work with?

Instead of being angry, getting distressed and telling everyone who will listen about your terrible boss spend your time and energy on becoming the type of colleague that you would rather work with. That type of person is one with integrity, kind, caring, compassionate and understanding. Killing your boss with kindness will strengthen your inner man as well as show your peers that you have the ability to stand under pressure.

Conclusion

So you are still alive! Your boss hasn't driven you to jump off a cliff yet? That's fantastic. Now I want to leave you with one last nugget, and that is to implement everything that you have learnt in this book. You see, one of man's greatest problems is that they are not doers. They love to talk a lot about doing but when it comes down to it things never get done. I can say this with confidence because there are very few successful people in the world, in fact, only 2 percent of the population own half of the worlds wealth, and that's because most people are not motivated enough to go after what they want. Since you have got to the end of this book, I am assuming that you want to become a part of that 2 percent, that elite group of people who do things differently than everyone else.

Wisdom is not having an abundance of knowledge. Wisdom is the application of the knowledge that you have. Have you ever met that person at a party who can tell you exactly how Bill Gates acquired his wealth but they are still complaining about not making it in life, and everyone is poor because of some big conspiracy theory that prevents the masses from acquiring wealth? People like this haven't applied the knowledge they have learnt.

So your boss is aggravating, the most annoying person in the world, hateful, mean and nasty, the question is what can you actually do about this? The answer is ABSOLUTELY NOTHING! If there is one thing I have learnt in life you can't change people, unless they themselves want to change, it's a waste of time trying. As you have read in this book, don't waste your energy moaning and complaining about them, simply focus on yourself and becoming the best person you can be and leave your evil boss to live in their evil world alone. Once you can wrap your mind around this concept, you will be skipping to work every day knowing that your joy can't be taken away from you.

Other books available by K.C. Smith on Kindle, paperback and audio:

Taking Destiny Steps: Learn How to Live Your Dreams

Everyone Screws Up: Learning To Forgive Your Stupid Mistakes and Recover With Grace and Humility

www.ingramcontent.com/pod-product-compliance
Lightning Source LLC
Chambersburg PA
CBHW030841180526
45163CB00004B/1411